AF431541

Thorns

IN HER FLESH

they say your thoughts
create your world
my third world was birthed
when the white storm
swept across our homesteads
do i get to recreate it
by simply thinking
of meadows and prairies
crystal jars
of milk and honey?

i think of thorns
pricking her beautiful skin
the midday sun
scorching her blooming day

i think of green fields and empty pots
flowing rivers and bare granaries
i think of beautiful jewels and plastic chains
naked servants and gucci clad masters
i think of flooded homes and empty dams
i think of the nail crowns
bleeding my people dry

~ *eshe*

Thorns

IN HER FLESH

ESHE BENSON

poems

thorns in her flesh

ISBN: 978-9914-704-90-7
Copyright © 2020 by Eshe Benson
www.eshebenson.com

All rights reserved. No part of this book publication may be reproduced, stored in a retrieval system, or transmitted in any way by any means, electronic, mechanical, photocopy, recording or otherwise without the prior permission of the copyright owner.

Published in 2020 by
Gems Publishing
P. O. Box 4083 – 00200
Nairobi

Illustrations by Christian Waweru, Shutterstock, Pixabay, Unsplash

other books by *eshe benson*
salt and gravity:
illustrated poems on pain, healing and self-love

follow *eshe* on social media:
facebook.com/eshepoems/
instagram.com/eshepoems

to my Maker
my Father
the Almighty God
what can i say?
without You i can do nothing

to my readers
you and i are the poem
i hope i keep writing us

to my family
you make dreaming possible
to my poet daughter Gem
your love for poetry rekindled in me
a fire i thought long dead
here we are

praise for eshe poems

"poems loaded with witty
and intelligently crafted messages"
David G.

"an interesting adventure
reading the poems"
James M.

"fun reading.
poetry like no other"
Cyrose Cyrose

"awesome content,
cannot let go of my copy"
Alex David

"amazing book"
Lucy Joseph

contents

thorns used to be my pricking companions
scarring me with black memories
that carried my echo to your nesting silence

you came riding on the morning breeze
and planted blooms

i love the blue blossoms
between my calm fingers
i love the orange blooms
crowning my florid head
i love how they bow phototaxically
towards your speckled light

~ *thorns in my flesh*

she tied the knot with the storm
said *i do* to the boisterous
breaking tides
she joined her heart
to the gushing river
consummated her love
to the slithering twister

she wedded
knowingly or unknowingly
the steel spade
the wet soil
burying her tired body
alive

~ she wedded the storm

sometimes i envy the wind
that gets to caress your face
the sun that gets to kiss your skin
when i cannot

~ *missing you*

pregnant blue clouds
beaded with arrogant crystals
whisper heavily into my spongy heart
chilling the ice-cold blood
flowing through my feminine veins

blue rain pouring on my frail form
each drop like a shepherd's whip
the excruciating pain
the only hope of
feeling again

from the other side of hell
she fed him killer mushrooms
then watched his face turn blue
he would rather die in her hands
than in the wild of his jungle

~ *killer mushrooms*

the gawking eyes
the covert looks
unashamedly following
our every move

judging miens
hateful glares
that quickly avert
when we look their way

their minds wonder
their thoughts speculate

i see through their transparent brains
i hear the whispers of confused souls

answer them
tell them

walk them through
our journey to here
open their eyes
with the sound of your voice
whisper
scream if you must
just tell them
put an end to these
endless appraisals

paint the colour of your blood
paint the colour of my blood
on a white canvas
let them tell you the difference
paint me white
paint you black

better still
paint me and you blue
i prefer blue aliens
in a black and white world
than the stares and sneers
than the whispers
concealing their disdain

answer them!
tell them!
will you?

~ tell them

the rain is tired of pouring on me
the sun is fed up with drying me

i dug a hole the size of his heart
bowed over and bled him into it
scrapped him from my skin
scooped him from my brain
sewed my heart
wrapped my skin
and walked away in stilts

~ *forgetting*

she used to warm herself
on your blazing fire
basking her young heart
under your glowing sun
your moon was all she needed
in the night
your star shined brightest
in her darkness

now your fire has grown cold
your sun is sprinkled with ice
your moon has gone into hiding
your star has fallen into the sea

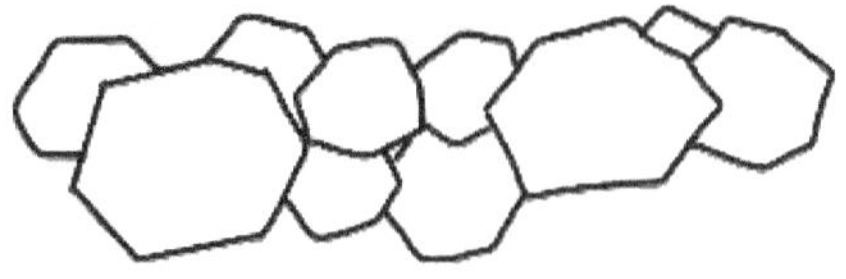

~ cold fires

she could have been his sun
to light his path
to far away meadows
he could not stand
her piercing brightness
he settled for the moon

the night came
the moon dimmed him further
he groped in the dark
and wished for the sun
only the sun was way beyond
the horizon of his past
quietly mooning over another
in a faraway land

~ he settled for the moon

her petals drip with honey
his bees gather water elsewhere

~ delinquent bees

the sun weeps grey tears
raining on the moon

lol
as in
love out loud
until the rain started pouring

she could not stand the pressure
he could not handle the measure

his thin filmy skin
could not take the poking
the prodding
the punching
the pricking
of their steel-nailed digits

her dear heart
was straining under the stakes
cracking
breaking
snapping with every insult

until in the end
the viscous blue romance
pooled at their feet
drowning them
in bitter-sweet memories

~ blue romance

you and me
the twinning of the moon and the sun

sordid floors
dark paths
lily scented nights
crispy country air
crackling fireplaces

shadows under the moon
sounds of the night
silence of the dark
mingling and tangoing
in perfect pitch
in harmonious beat
of intoxicating drums
and twirling dance
of dizzying village love

~ *village love*

the ill-tempered brutes come out in line
neigh and bow before her slight majesty
like gentle mules with no stomping strength

she knots their fluffy tails
sets them on orange fire
unleashing their savage spirits
into her burning wild

~ *she sure can woo them*

i believed he was made only for me
he believed he was God's gift to all

is my mind playing old tricks on me?
or has your colour changed?
i saw you walking down middle street
you looked all white
prim and proper

now at the setting of the sun
at the crawling out of the moon
your full colours seem to bloom
burgeoning before
the nakedness of my watch

you have changed
into a fusion
of improper browns and greys
you have even thrown in
some complimentary black

~ *full colours*

his big heart fell from the clouds
shattered into a thousand pieces
terrazzo grains scattered
across the concrete floor
smearing red stains
on her white satin dress
flakes of his flesh
stuck to her virgin feet
he walked away
and got sucked into the storm

~ heartbreak

she danced on grey moon
for your dim eyes
sang your tickling songs
to deaf birds

she carried your fiery sun
on her gaunt shoulders
felt your clumsy weight
on her weary back

she held your bleeding hurt
in her soft heart
cried your burning tears
with her tired eyes

she spent wide-eyed nights
for your sleep
waited her life away
for your arrival

today she sits on the ashes
of your burning pride
while you perch your rainbows
on top of the world

~ waiting for your arrival

extended blue veins
straining against
my flimsy translucent skin
taut as dry wood
threatening to shred
to break in free eruption
into bloody black rivulets

~ anxiety

which revolving door
have you strode through?
where have your hands been?

the shadow of his night lingers
the sun is afraid of it

~ stuck

he emptied her
drained her of herself
one day she floated away
to find herself

36

the accusations flying
across your taut face
are as clear as september sky
the deep sadness
of your thoughtful eyes
crushing the core
of a heart weak for you

i do not know why yet
but the pain in your eyes
reminds me so vividly
of my sweet mother's breast

i look up to her smiling face
nestling comfortably
on her soft bosom
i suckle one soft nipple
the supple tissue tickling
my swollen gum

i need to nibble
bite something
the soft flesh of her generous tit
has become my treasured toy

i press harder this time
the pleasure too irresistible
i am stopped abruptly
by a sharp slap
on my small tender thigh

i have pushed the limits i know
things just got out of hand

but i swear by my mother's breast
i never meant to cause you pain

~ *by my mother's breast*

what are you doing here?
his name is boldly emblazoned
on your forehead

he told me i was crass
he told me i was trash
he told me i had no fire
he told me he was tired
he told me
he was leaving me for her

perched on the window
of my empty lair
with a half sneer parked
on my dry lips
i watched their cute
garden wedding
as they strolled on the
jacaranda carpet

today
she tearfully knocked on my door

he told her she was crass
he told her she was trash
he told her she had no fire
he told her he was tired
he told her
he was leaving her for her

~ they came home to roost

you know they were right
when you see his new garden
watered and full of blooms

~ move on

i love all colours
the golden orange of the setting sun
the red of young roses in bloom
the green of the virgin plains in spring
i love all colours
except the blue hues
painted over my lonely heart

the purple carpet of jacaranda blooms
the white blanket of clouds
over a new april day
the yellow hues of the morning sun
i love all colours
except the blue storm
raging over my aching heart

the crystal water rushing down the river
the white of snow-capped tropical mountain
the soft red earth under my tired feet
i love all colours
except the heavy blue shades
of missing you

~ *i love all colours*

wilting flowers
never smelt so great

i see your beautiful smile
on the face of a stranger
i hear your soft voice
in the whistling wind of my restless mind
i hear your soothing laughter
in the mingled noises of a boisterous day
i hear your heartbeat
in the heavy thumping of my aching heart

~ this love!

his acid sweat burns cavernous holes
through her delicate skin
rancid fumes from the fireplace
waft across her hazed mind
fogging her melting brain

his heart turns sooty under her glaring watch
his icy breath like midnight rain
upon her frozen face
this apparition from a distant land
is slowly becoming
a noxious reality

the wanton feats
the merry laughter
the rash manners
now graduating
with hats too brimmed to be real
all so quietly with no beating drums
into this dull
calm
collected
yawning
organized love

come drift with me to the mountaintops
come dance with me on the treetops
come sing with me in the raindrops
i will make it worth
your dreamy while

she got him dancing
to the beats of wind
she got him singing
empty melodies from clogged lungs
she got him longing
for meadows and prairies
she got him dreaming
of ocean tides and boisterous seas
she got him talking
of forever and ever

then
she got him taking
lonely strolls in the dark of night
she got him shouting unutterables
in his heavy head
she got him fighting
to get out of his morning bed
she got him shedding blue rivers
in the winter rain

~ she sure got him

bleeding threads
cascading down his wall
a canvas of apparitions
a mural of nightmares
a smiling feminal phantom

~ memories

she descends majestically
her crystals glistening
as she lands ever so gently
on the beaded dust
mingled with the wafting scent
of kilned earth

the parched ground opens its thirsty lips
to welcome the dripping of life
into its bosom
a dry blade of grass rises to attention
aroused by the gentle beating
upon its back

just as quickly as she appeared
she lifts
her glistening beads leave the unsated air
the dry earth still panting with want
longing for just one sip
of intoxicating
summer rain

empty rooms
filled with nothingness
in the dead of a humid night
the absurdity of it all
invoking blue laughter
from the dry recesses
of her broken heart
like old oil dripping
from an abandoned mine
gushing unrestrained
from her cracked angry lips

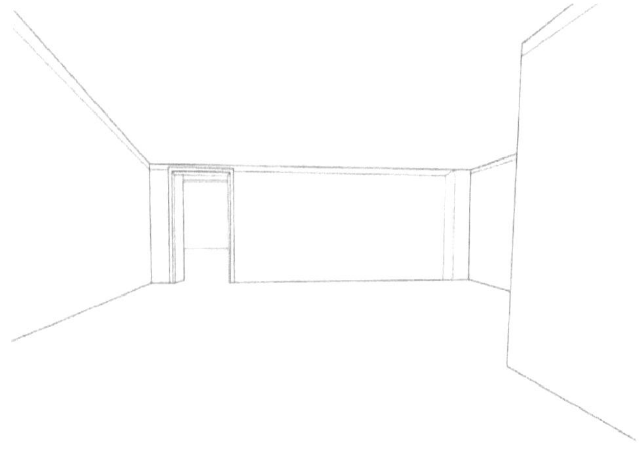

~ emptiness

he searched for her among the roses
she looked for him among the mosses
somewhere along the way
they missed themselves

coursing through every cell
running down
invading my every sense
like the liquid blood
flowing through my feminine veins
bathing and immersing
my entire being

~ *liquid love*

hyena dance

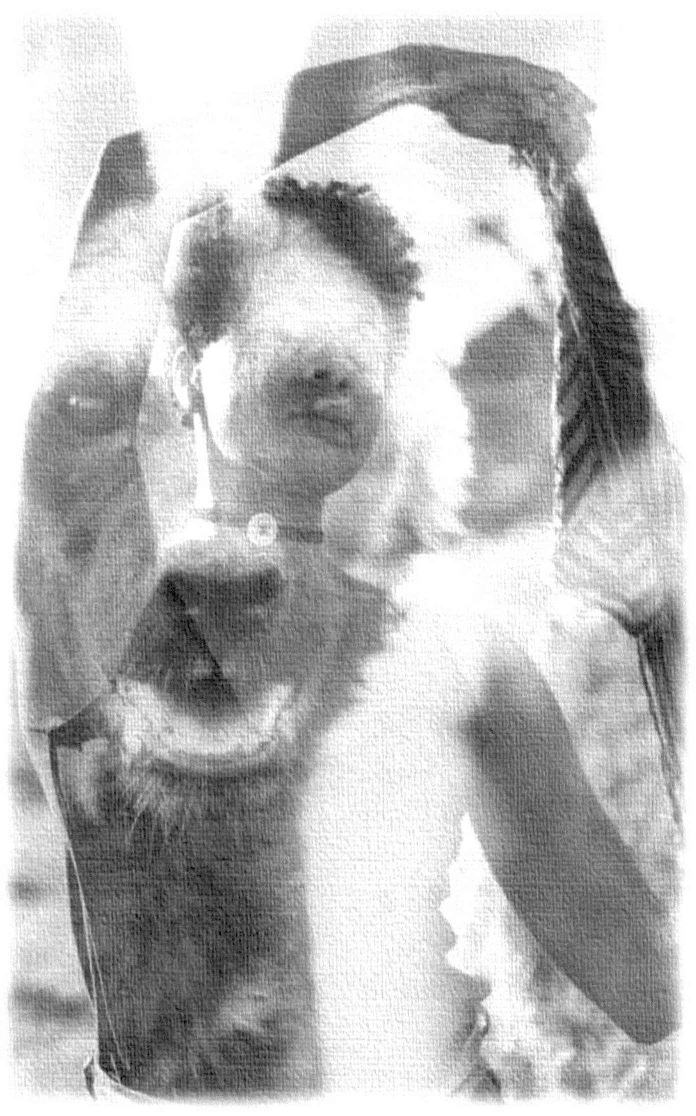

they say your thoughts
create your world
my third world was birthed
when the white storm
swept across our homesteads
do i get to recreate it?
by simply thinking
of meadows and prairies
crystal jars
of milk and honey?

i think of thorns
pricking her beautiful skin
the midday sun
scorching her blooming day

i think of green fields and empty pots
flowing rivers and bare granaries
i think of beautiful jewels and plastic chains
naked servants and gucci clad masters
i think of flooded homes and empty dams
i think of the nail crowns
bleeding my people dry

~ thoughts from my world

mama did not know
my name betrays me
she would have given me a proper noun
to pompously tag on my proper name

one that would not betray my blood
one that would not deny my kin
one that would secure my plight
one that would be tolerable to rank

~ my name betrays me

protracted gobbling tentacles
straining life out of the gaunt necks
of his hungry subjects

like a dry parched earth
an abyss that is never full
he guzzles down the blood and sweat
of his unwilling prey

a deep gaping pit
an arrogant conduit of all life's finery
flowing unmetered
to his bottomless form
while his trusting subjects
gawk enviously

his victims lie limp
like dead leaves ready to rot
shells of dead wood
long-gone souls
not knowing they created
the monster eating them

~ *corruption*

give some
to get some
the ladder is shorter
if you do
the journey is longer
if you do not
skirts get shorter
brains shrink smaller

~ it is a dogs' world

they call her
the dark continent
though the sun shines
brightest on her
blue rain pours on her
every day
making nonsense
of her sun's toil

the twirling tails
the thumping feet
confusing and scaring
the most brave

i am afraid
but fearlessly i dance
to the rhythm
of confused intentions
of man and man-eater's
midday dance

the lingering scent
of my flesh and blood
temptingly wafts over
to their hungry senses

i refuse to become their next meal
i dance till the dawn
of the man-made jungle

the dance becomes a slow waltz
their tongues hang out
with exhausted passions

i keenly watch their zombie moves
intoxicated by the wine
of their unstated greed
until they fall over
into a long unwise slumber

~ hyena dance

on the coloured blind
of your pitiful mind
your blood looks white
my blood looks black

~ colour blind

his formal gait
tailored to impress confidence
his steady gaze
designed to echo thoughtfulness
his handpicked words
organized to sound wise
his slight smile
curated to look important
his perfect suit
styled with hooks to your brain

~ *designer life*

"*dark continent*"
tattooed across her bold behind
in black dripping ink
devoid of white drapes
to the amusement of drunks

"poverty"
etched on her ebony back
in bright golden crayons
bought from the white shop
across her brown mud hut

"corrupt"
branded across her parched hands
a constant reminder
that her sin is more glowing
than the white-washed guilt of *west*

"backward"
imprinted on her firm breast
her suckling tot would have to see
that years spent in white servitude
rendered her less human

"foolish"
stamped on her pleated brow
with black indelible ink
to match her dark skin and white brain
bereft of a white education

ALGERIA
LIBYA
UNITED ARAB REPUBLIC
SAUDI ARABIA
IRAQ
TUNISIA
MALI
NIGER
CHAD
SUDAN
Khartoum
UPPER VOLTA
DAHOMEY
TOGO
GHANA
NIGERIA
CAMEROON
CENTRAL AFRICAN REPUBLIC
ETHIOPIA
EQUATORIAL GUINEA
GABON
REP OF CONGO
DEMOCRATIC REPUBLIC OF THE CONGO
UGANDA
Kampala
KENYA
Nairobi
RWANDA
BURUNDI
TANZANIA
Dar es Salaam
Luanda
ANGOLA
MALAWI
ZAMBIA
Lusaka
MOZAMBIQUE
SOUTH WEST AFRICA
Windhoek
WALVIS BAY
BOTSWANA
Gaberones
Pretoria
SWAZILAND
REPUBLIC OF SOUTH AFRICA
LESOTHO

~africa

he struggles and gasps
longing to fill his frail lungs
with just a short gust
of now precious air

he writhes and twists
groaning inaudibly
in confusion and pain
his chest feels tight
his small form
weak with exhaustion

instinctively
unwittingly
he opens his small unused mouth
he swallows and chokes
on the thick fluid
that was once
his source of life

a battle is raging
in what was once
his peaceful home
his world is churning
his being is in turmoil
he is drowning
in a fast receding ocean
of a dark unfamiliar world
then suddenly
everything stops
he takes one last breath
of goodbye to the world
he never got to know

of the cuddle he never got to get
of the laughter he never got to share
of a life he never got to live

~ a life never lived

his gashing wounds bleed from within
his silent moans audible to none
his tears unseen
his cries unheard

the rat-race has taken its toll
the society is his final judge
what he makes proves him a man
who he is does not count
what he drives must be bigger
than his bleeding heart

he has nothing
if he is not spinning the latest
he is a nobody
if he has not perched his
adorable family on the leafy suburbs
he is nonentity
if his adorable brood
is not schooling with princes
he is insignificant
if his beautiful wife
is not driving the sleekest

~ *middle class*

dropping temples
drooping miens
parched skins
calloused palms
sinewy muscles
hardened lips
wearied souls
roughened feet
a rainbow of emotions
a tapestry of thoughts

~ *toughened ways*

i hear the laughter
drifting from happy children
from the homesteads where mama works
the *mwangis* and the *okellos*
they have it all she says
i wonder what she means by that

mama says
mwangi's daughter *rachel* is my age
i would like to see her someday
though mama said *no*
i often wonder where she goes to school
what her school is like

mama says
she is very tired today
she talked about scrubbing and cooking
she also talked about the pink bedroom
belonging to *rachel*
i wonder how it would feel like
to have my own bedroom

mama says
we are blessed
to have a roof over our heads
even though when it rains
it is like the roof is not there
would we not be more blessed
with a roof that does not leak

or two rooms
with a good roof over our heads?

mama says
okello's children are wasteful
am not sure i understand
there is hardly enough at home
she says we should not complain
after all i get to go to school
there we get to have a meal

mama says
one day our lives will be like theirs
we will have our own home and enough to eat
i believe her
i want to believe her
i pray for her
i pray for my siblings

~ *domestic worker*

is it the emptying of my mind
for *western* ideals?
or the adding to my ideals
what is good from the *west?*

~ *modern education*

last night my brother did not come home
mama waited the whole night
i wanted to wait with her but i fell asleep
i dreamt she was crying
and praying softly

mama woke up earlier than usual today
i doubt she slept at all
her eyes look red
the way they used to look
every morning daddy came home

daddy no longer comes home
mama says he went to heaven
when he drank something bad
i wonder if daddy fights in heaven
the way he used to fight us
mama says you cannot do bad things in heaven

i can tell mama is worried for my brother
she does not want him to go to heaven yet
she wants him to go back to school
i would also like to see him back in school
mama says my brother does not like school
i do not know if she knows the truth
i heard him tell his friends
he does not mind school
but he needs to work
to help her with rent and food
i wonder if my brother will ever come home

my friend *allan* told me
what happened to his brother

bad people stabbed him as he walked home
i wonder if *allan's* brother is in heaven
i wonder if he has met daddy

i do not want my brother
to go to heaven and meet daddy
even though mama says
heaven is a happy place
mama and i need him
more than God and daddy
please God bring my brother home
today

~ ghetto gloom

i stand boldly
in rank and wit
before the midday sun
the noise
of my tempestuous blood
is louder
than *johnny's* flour mill

you have padded your ears
to the sound of my misery
you have put blinders
against the silhouette
of my unwelcome existence

my screams
stain your clear day
my words
defile your peaceful night

i haunt your dreams
i gnaw at your conscious

you wish me away
then wake up to find me
seated heavily
on your padded chair

you see
it took me long to get here
it will take you longer
to get me going

~ *here to stay*

strutting on neon heels
down *cabro-paved* streets
my head in the clouds
my nose in the air
my chin on top
of the city evergreens
my neck getting longer
with every back-twisting stride
i am on butterfly wings
i am the wispy feather
of a blithe eagle

he has cooked
fed our growing brood
scrubbed the mirror kitchen
he sits with his large heart
in his fishing boots
staring unseeingly
at the large screen
his waders are shrinking
his heart is sinking

he hopes i am okay
he prays i am okay
he dreads the night
i will not be okay

he is choking
on the hot potato
of my freedom

my stilettos are breaking

under the weight of my head
in rancid silence
we eat our burnt goose

~ the goose is overcooked

he snakes through the heavy morning traffic
like a swift provoked cobra
out on a hunting mission
pursuing a fast and furious prey

he does not care for any rules or laws
no direction is forbidden
he crisscrosses all the four lanes
behind and ahead of speeding motorists

the luggage of willing humans
bundled in multiples the law forbids
swaying left and right
hanging by the grip
of *boda madness*

*(boda boda – motor bikes used in africa and the
developing world as means of public transport)*

we drink from their calabash full of lies
feast from the stinking pot
of putrid deception
brewed in the minds and meets
of our so-called leaders

the charging buffaloes hook their twisted horns
through our scrawny bellies
dragging our pitiful selves
through maniacal episodes
of euphoric chest thumping
maddening bouts
of pretentious mudslinging
every election year

dazed from knocking our heads
on walls erected for this purpose
we gladly sell our souls
and blindly give our votes
offering them yet another chance
to empty our coffers
into their ever-growing pockets
and ever-enlarging bellies

we then watch in self-pity
as our scrawny children
and malnourished elders
strangle under the grip of hunger
our sick dying of curable maladies

while our kith and kin
spend cold unrelenting nights
in makeshift wooden sheds

and torn metal shacks
unfit for human habitation

~ putrid deception

five pairs of hungry eyes
stare dreamingly at my pained face
unseen fingers like sharp nails
pierce unrelentingly
punching holes on my bleeding heart

i plead my innocence
i beg for mercy
they do not seem to care
all they know is the gnawing pain
of their empty bellies
the sound of their rumbling stomachs

i accept the poking
the pain
bind my bleeding hurt
and stare into the black pot
its empty belly defiantly stares back
i place my heavy head
in my rugged hands
and cry

~ *empty pot*

step up and speak to my bold face
unwrap you brains before my fed-up self
drool your words on your proud chest
let me see the lettery cascade of your bile
the storm behind your pretentious smile

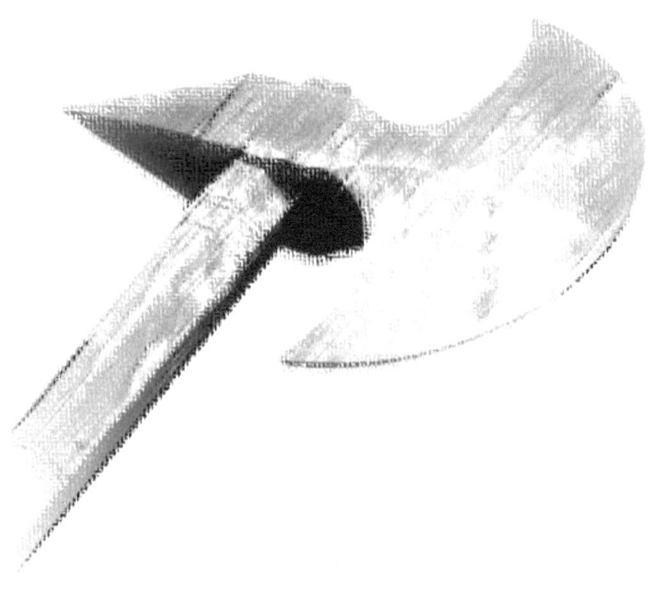

~ backstabbing

somebody
wake me
shake me
rouse me
from yesterday's dream

yesterday
the rain was generous
the farms were lush
the harvest was heavy
the barns were full

yesterday
there was enough for all and more
the cat and rat ate together
the rich and poor dined like kings
the farmer walked through his farm
a rare twinkle in his quick eyes

today
the earth is scorched dry
dehydrated animals collapse at the roadsides
weary farmers wobble in want
malnourished children play with thin dust
scrawny wives stare into the horizon
dreaming of yesterday

a loving mother
carried an angel in her womb
nine months of tears and joy
anticipation mingled with fear

on the momentous day
he was delivered
to her uncertain world
she looked at his small form
and wept

at six years
the angel came of age
with searing pain she let go
of the one she loved
in a way only she could

street urchin
in *kenya*
chokora is his name
the name given
to her precious son

faceless body
dripping with black odor
black clothes
gleaming in the sun
a beautiful soul
hidden way beneath
nobody seems to know

nobody seems to care
that deep within

the faceless form
is the little angel
she birthed and loved

~ chokora (street urchin)

the placid rot of yesterday's blooms
conceal wet mounds of infested soils
amorphous sheaths
cover unmarked graves
hide bloodsucking tentacles
that leech off inordinate hungry souls
eating flesh and swallowing dreams

~ *politics*

several eyes
stare in unusual alertness
distrust and curiosity play out
on the innocent faces
their small dry mouths fall open
unwittingly betraying
the unsaid words
the feelings of wonder
the sense of admiration
the longing
for just a flitting contact
with the stranger and her coupé

with one sweep of my eyes
i take it all in
the stench
the garbage
the muck
at the front and back alleys
of rotten iron sheet structures
not fit for human habitation
but home to millions of *kenyans*
who do not know any other life

i say a feeble hello
to the now smiling faces
of the faceless children
sons and daughters
of our merciless land
like a ghost in daylight

i pause then pass
as i wonder in silent guilt

how such darkness
has not been obliterated
by the sun hanging
over our leafy suburbs

~ dark age

her wrinkled hands
scooped and sewed up my womanhood
presented the flakes of my tender gift
on a golden platter
for the elders' approval
i was now a woman

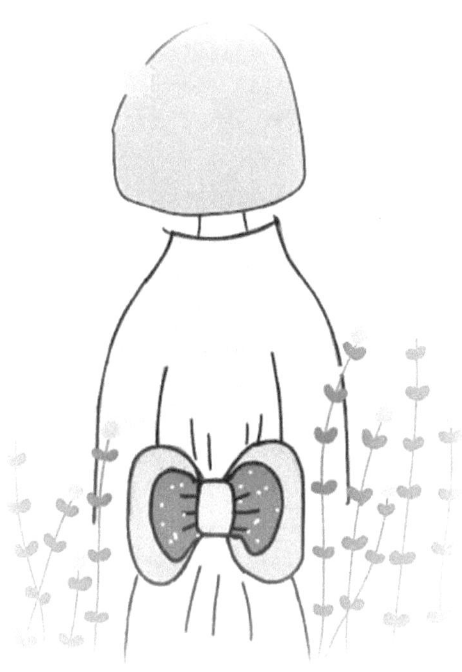

~ *fgm*

tangled knot

baby coos from the bare pink nursery
drift noiselessly
into the lifeless neighborhood
barnacled tentacles clutch my dry pipes
i swallow the tentacles
they turn bitter in my brooding bowels
pungent sweat drips down my pleated brow

i clutch the shreds of my shattered heart
in the veined palm of my trembling hand
i hurl it fiercely against the staring walls
my grainy heart mates with the ice-cold walls
and breaks into blue rhymes
to sooth the wounded hollow
of my broken heart

~ *blue rhymes*

unrestrained
un-tempered
he is a child of the wind

she clutches her heart
in her wrinkled hands
he carries his head
in his tired palms
the child floats
above their crouched forms

~ *trouble child*

he nursed on her venom tit
his bile has risen
his tongue fills his mouth

~ toxic parenting

humid noxious air
dripping gunk
drilling through her fresh skin
muffling the sound of rough cottons
as her mind wanders

her eyeballs fix on a spot
a moment
a ray in the horizon of her existence
her curled fingers wriggle
and reach out to a time and a place
conceived and pregnant
in the womb of her mind

he rolls away
sighing with throaty noises
with only his rusty scent
to bring her back from neverland

~ *kin (un)love*

the nursery man said they were tomato seeds
with a self-assured grin
he watered them with the sweat of his brow
fertilised the soil with the juice of his toil

everyone knows tomatoes are red
right?

only they turned out to be rogue tomatoes
no way he could have slaved to breed
these black-streaked monsters

~ *rogue tomatoes*

where she used to grow greens
to feed her adorable angels
black blossoms now bloom
their twines covering the ground
black petals swaying softly
in the grey breeze of day

she tends the blossoms
religiously
their musky scent
massaging her weary senses
crusty teardrops glistening
on her wrinkled face
blue memories
flooding her aging mind

it seems just like yesterday
they were a young bubbly lot
she could have sworn
before the Almighty
she had done right
with them

then the black wind
that unrelenting storm
swept mercilessly
across her dusty homestead
burying them all
next to each other

the black blossoms
stoically taking their place

~ black blossoms

twisted untangle-able knots
of all colours
running through our skins
our brains
our blood
tying us intricately and haphazardly
a complex mass of tight ropes
cording me
you
in an endless dance of life
and i wonder
death?

~ *kin*

her crusty blue brush
paints all colours black
her looming grey clouds
cover the sun

she kills slowly
softly but sure
like dripping mercury
like drooling acid
flowing lazily
from a broken pot
drilling icy holes
eating up flesh
drowning life
bleeding air
out of the lungs
of the living

~ cantankerous woman

guttural rending
wrenching animal groans
the inexplainable crashing pain
of her shredding insides
churning
violently breaking
as the smallest of humans
seeks to break free
from the safe prison
of her motherly protection

~ *motherhood*

he creeps in unnoticed
veiled in saintly regalia
into the lives of those we love
at first their friendship
is easy and cordial
sip after sip
the friendship scales start to tip
from mutual to dependency
from easy to demanding

thoughts of their next encounter
preoccupy him
his limbs get weak
his head gets heavy
he sets out in a dazed state of regret
to look for his daily companion

his coffers are empty
well-wishers come in handy
or payback of a favor owed
he gulps down the dark brown liquid
or the clear illegal fluid
depending on the day's fortunes

he wakes up drenched
somewhere in a trench
stinking muck
flowing over his weak self
he throws up
into the passing effluent

the stench hanging onto him
his insides churning within

i need help
he mutters to himself
for the millionth time
but first to *wambui's* den
tomorrow is as good a day
to seek it
little does he know
for him and his buddies
tomorrow will never be

~ vicious friend

do not be fooled
by her white smile
contrasted by ebony skin
do not judge this book
by the cover of her pages

do not be duped
by her full-figured swagger
her hearty laughter
seemingly of no care

her heart is strong
her love is vibrant
her rage as boisterous
as her stormy mirth

she will fight if she must
she will run because she must
she will stay
because she wants
to love you in the storm

her heart
like an angel
her wrath
a gathering storm
her smile
a soothing balm
her grip
as strong as a vise

her touch
a baby's sigh

her limbs
swift as a deer
her love
a gentle breeze

~ the ebony force

bitter heart
bitter thoughts
bitter words
dripping
pouring like october rain
pooling languidly
like an old toxic well
sending back putridness
killing the master
and subject alike

~ bitterness

i dance to the beat of her song
twirl to the whoosh of her skirts
i elatedly belt out her carefree tune
smile at the touch of her breeze
i sigh at her whisper of my name

she lifts and tosses me in the air
i giggle with delight
at the touch of freedom
just to land shamefacedly on the ground
never to trust the wind again

~ *the luring wind*

he threw the pot against the wall
she slowly bounced back
she stubbornly lives

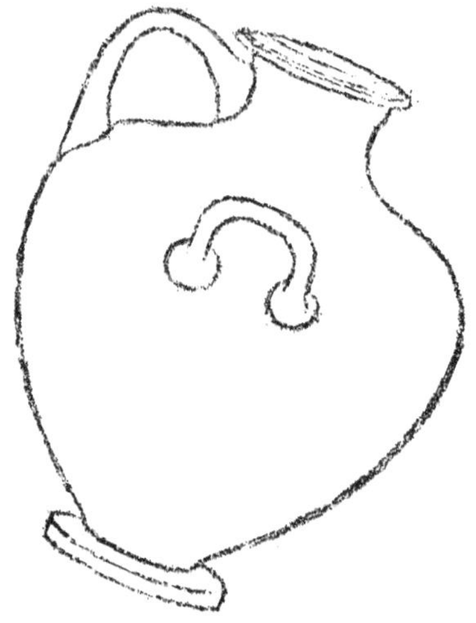

~ unbreakable

they flow down long ebony necks
in all colours textures and lengths
curly
straight
long
short
black
blond
brown
red
some natural
others quite unreal and eccentric
against the gleaming ebony skins
of stunning *african* queens

~ *hair weaves*

liquid fire

in the closet of her hungry mind
she weaved lofty dreams
rainbow threads
towering and mounting
pregnant mosaics of her restless mind
resplendent tapestries of her fertile wit
she stepped back and loved the colours

then she slept
a tooth-full smile stuck between her lips

then she dreamt
a dream that would take her to wits end
a spotted incorrigible hyena
with snorting laughter on his lips
was peeing rabidly
on her rainbow dreams

~ he peed on her dreams

i caught my foot on treetops
spinning reeds with weaver birds
when i could have been
flapping wings with eagle birds

her fire was locked away
in tempered glass bottles
she steamed
under her own sweat
she was burning
in her own blaze
one day she wriggled and stood
taller than the oak tree
in her backyard
the bottles shattered
sending fireworks into the night
butterflies danced
under her bright light
fireflies twirled
with her colorful sparks

~ *fire in a bottle*

do not struggle to untangle me
i was not meant to be understood
i am eternity stretched beyond time
what is mortal cannot unravel the eternal

i am not the colour of my skin
i am not the shape of my nose
i am not the sound of my name
i am not the size of my brain
i cannot fit in the mold of your taxonomy

the ocean belly hides much
below her fleeting surface
only her Maker knows her depth
you cannot measure my eternal essence
with a span of your rational eyes
the lingering attempts to unstitch me

i am beyond the limits of your mind
i am beyond the sphere of your kind
what is mortal cannot unravel the eternal

~ stretch of eternity

she walked with roosters
long enough to see
chicken speckles on her eagle face

deep down the village alley
camouflaged by dark shadows
of impervious moonless nights
young girls lose their virginity
as easily and as fast
as baffled farmers
lose their arrow roots
to the village wag

deep down the dark belly
of the village alley
young men snort away
dull evenings and bright futures
losing their innocence
to illicit pleasures
and illegal substances

deep down the village alley
yesterday's dreams
have become
impossible mirages
for today's youth
the village alley has now become
the infamous alley of lost dreams

~ *the village alley*

mama taught me
not to drag my feet
as i walk through the sands of time
a thirsty soul might come looking
and find their way
to the watering hole

~ *footprints*

silent moans
inaudible groans
held back
in empty tombs
of regrets
of what-ifs
of what could have been
but is not

~ *tombs of what-ifs*

i look down
at the obscure pool of dreams
lying below my straddled legs
like tattered un-shapely garments
plastered with aged sweat streaks
dripping with dry tears
broken threads running bare
across the old rugs
that were once beautiful tapestries
carried across many oceans
to the land of empty dreams

~ broken dreams

i am a butterfly
i am changing
and it is okay

~ *growing*

she livened the world with her songs
one day the hippo heard her sing
he looked up and insulted her beak
she stared at her reflection in the water
the hippo was right
she was one ugly fowl
she was one ungifted bird

she swore never to come out again
she swore never to sing again

while she sits still
the world is silent
waiting for nightingale to sing

each time she fell she grew

wide eyed
tails wagging
ears straining
slyly they tiptoe around me
soundlessly circling my privacy
picking potent seeds
scattered within my busy wits
i wake up to lush fields
planted and growing
seeded with my secret dreams

~ the apes

does my candle dim your light?

grass grows under her heavy feet
she refuses to move
until he comes to mow
and move her

~ mind sets

thorns in her flesh is an illustrated collection of poems by a black woman on love that is often like a rose flower; magnificent in its beauty but burdened with pricking thorns.

it is also about the realities of family relationships and the socio-cultural, spiritual, economic, and political complexities of life in the *african* context.

in this collection of poetry, *eshe* has thrown together poems of different themes; something akin to mixing lemon slices and balls of sugar in water. she hopes you, her dear reader, would be kind enough to stir and enjoy a tall glass of lemonade!

the book is split into four chapters: pricking companions, hyena dance, tangled knots, and liquid fire.

~ *about the book*

eshe benson is a poet, author, and entrepreneur on a lifelong mission to inspire, empower, uplift, and entertain people through the power of storytelling. she also strives to shift rigid perspectives and paradigms that no longer serve humanity.

hailing from a tiny kenyan village where a good education was only possible for a few privileged villagers, eshe refused to let the odds that were stacked up against her stand in her way. she went on to earn a bachelor's degree, a master of science degree in entrepreneurship, a doctorate in biblical studies, and two post-graduate diplomas. on top of all her hard work in the academic arena, she merged her passion for empowerment and poetry and created two books: "thorns in her flesh" and "salt and gravity".

when she isn't pouring her heart out onto paper or a computer screen, you can find this fun-loving writer going on epic adventures around the world, dancing like nobody's watching, and cooking tasty meals.

to find about more about eshe, take a look at her official website: www.eshebenson.com

~ about the author

mama taught me
not to drag my feet
as i walk through the sands of time
a thirsty soul might come looking
and find their way
to the watering hole

~ eshe

thank you for reading this book.
if you enjoyed it, kindly take a moment
to leave a review at your favorite retailer.

also follow *eshe* on social media :
eshe benson facebook page
eshe benson instagram page

or visit her website:
www.eshebenson.com

other books by *eshe benson*
salt and gravity:
illustrated poems on pain, healing and self-love

www.ingramcontent.com/pod-product-compliance
Lightning Source LLC
Chambersburg PA
CBHW020525160726
47992CB00005BA/2259